JBIOG
Peter
Stanley, Diane

Peter the Great

PETER the GREAT

by Diane Stanley

Four Winds Press • New York   Collier Macmillan Publishers • London

The author wishes to acknowledge the following books as her chief sources in the preparation of the text and illustrations for this book:

Afanasév, Aleksandr Nikolaevich. *Russian Folk Tales*. Illustrated by Ivan I. Bilibin. Boston: Shambhala Publications, Inc., 1980.

Ascher, Abraham. "The Kremlin." *Newsweek*, 1978.

Bortoli, Georges. *Moscow and Leningrad Observed*. New York: Oxford University Press, 1975.

Buzzi, Giancarlo. *The Life and Times of Peter the Great*. Curtis Publishing Co., 1967.

Massie, Robert K. *Peter the Great, His Life and World*. New York: Ballantine Books, 1981.

Onassis, Jacqueline, ed. *In the Russian Style*. New York: Viking Penguin, Inc., 1976.

Putnam, Peter. *Peter, the Revolutionary Tsar*. New York: Harper & Row, 1973.

Wallace, Robert. *The Rise of Russia*. New York: Time, Inc., 1967.

Four Winds Press
Macmillan Publishing Company
866 Third Avenue, New York, N.Y. 10022
Collier Macmillan Canada, Inc.
Printed and bound in Japan
First American Edition

10   9   8   7   6   5   4   3

The text of this book is set in 14 pt. Fairfield.
The illustrations are rendered in gouache.
Library of Congress Cataloging-in-Publication Data
Stanley, Diane. Peter the Great.
Summary: A biography of the tsar who began the
transformation of Russia into a modern state in the
late seventeenth-early eighteenth centuries.
1. Peter I, Emperor of Russia, 1672-1725—Juvenile
literature. 2. Soviet Union—Kings and rulers—Biography—
Juvenile literature. 3. Soviet Union—History—
Peter I. 1689-1725—Juvenile literature. [1. Peter I,
Emperor of Russia, 1672-1725. 2. Kings, queens, rulers,
etc. 3. Soviet Union—History—Peter I, 1689-1725] I. Title.
DK131.S78   1986   947'.05'0924 [B] [92]   85-13060
ISBN 0-02-786790-0

This book is lovingly dedicated
to the memory of
CARL ISAAC SHULMAN
1917–1984

It was spring in the year 1685.

In the hush of dawn the soldiers crept noiselessly to their positions, their weapons loaded. Within minutes they would attack the fort below them on the banks of the quiet river.

Peter crouched beside his cannon awaiting the command to fire.

The command came. With a dreadful blast, mortars and cannons pounded the fort, shattering it and sending wood and earth flying. With whoops of triumph the soldiers clambered over the wreckage and claimed complete victory.

Miles away, already hard at work in the fields, peasants heard the noise and grumbled, "There's the tsar, playing his games again!"

It was true. The soldier who fired his cannon with such excitement was Peter Alexeevich, tsar of all Russia and her eight million people. And, though tall for his age, he was only a boy of thirteen, playing soldiers.

Like any spoiled child, Peter believed that whatever he wanted, he should have, and the sooner the better. As a little boy, he had trained monkeys and dancing bears to entertain him. A whole staff of dwarves waited on him.

When he grew older and wanted to play soldier, he was given his own army of children, complete with barracks to live in, uniforms to wear, and plenty of muskets and cannons to make noise with. All his life he would want fantastic things, and want them right away.

Most boys who happened to be kings and to have an army of children to play with, would make themselves commander-in-chief. But Peter never did, either as a child or as a man. He assigned himself the lowest rank and worked his way up. He slept, ate, and worked with the other boys, expecting no special treatment. Peter always believed that honors should be earned through learning and hard work, not handed out to people because they were rich or important.

Russia was vast, the largest nation on earth. It spread from Europe on the west to the Pacific Ocean on the east. In Europe, wonderful things were happening: Scientists, explorers, painters, musicians, and writers were changing their world.

But the Russians did not wish to change. They firmly believed that the old ways were best and that life should continue as it had been in their fathers', and their grandfathers', and their great-grandfathers' time. They did not wish to visit Europe to see the exciting new discoveries, and they did not wish for Europeans to visit them. The Russians simply wished to be left alone.

There were, however, a few Europeans living in Russia as advisors to the government, most of them to help run the army.

They were not permitted to live among the Russians and were kept together in a settlement called the "German suburb." They weren't all Germans, of course, but the Russians never could tell one European from another.

This elegant little European town had grand mansions along tree-lined avenues, little parks with splashing fountains, and, most of all, *Europeans*. These modern men and women dressed in the stylish mode of the day, read foreign books, and entertained one another at dinner parties where they talked about marvelous things.

Peter knew many of them, for they were his teachers in military matters. He couldn't believe how different their world was from that of Russia. He thought their world was wonderful. How he wished *his* country could be like theirs!

9

One summer day, Peter and an old Dutchman were visiting one of the country houses belonging to the royal family. In a shed they discovered an old boat. Peter had never seen anything like it.

"Timmerman!" called Peter. "What do you make of this?"

"It looks like an English sailboat, sir."

"Why is it shaped like that? What does it do?"

The Dutchman smiled and opened his eyes very wide in amusement. "Why, it can sail into the wind—upstream!"

"Is it possible?" Peter cried. "Can you sail it? Can *you* make it do that?"

"I'll find you someone who can, after it's fixed up a bit. It will need a new mast, and some sails, and some patching here and there."

When, at last, the boat was launched in the river, Peter watched breathlessly as it tacked back and forth upstream into the wind. After that, Peter spent every spare moment learning to sail. And on those sun-filled days Peter's vision of the future began to take shape. He dreamed of more boats, bigger boats. Someday, Russia must have a navy and a port to put it in.

The young boy was growing into a man. Soon he would no longer play games; he would be ready to begin his life's work: bringing Russia into the modern world.

Peter spent more and more time in the German suburb as the years passed. He dressed like the Europeans and tried to imitate their ways. What he longed for, more than anything else in the world, was to see Europe for himself. There was so much to learn!

He decided to do what no Russian tsar had ever done: He would travel to the West. But he would not travel in glory as the head of the great embassy, wasting precious time at tiresome parties and receptions in his honor. He would leave all that to Francis Lefort, his ambassador. Peter planned to travel disguised as a common soldier. As he now stood six feet, seven inches tall, however, and carried himself with great authority, it was easy to recognize him.

Before he left, Peter had a seal engraved for himself that read, "I am a pupil and need to be taught."

In the spring of 1697 a grand procession of sledges, carriages, and wagons left Russia, carrying to the West 250 men—the ambassador, noblemen, priests, soldiers, clerks, cooks, and musicians who made up the embassy. They carried with them a huge quantity of sable furs with which they would pay their expenses. These men would be gone from all that was familiar to them for a year and a half, visiting Latvia, Poland, Germany, and Austria, but especially Holland and England, where Peter wanted to study shipbuilding.

It was the talk of Europe. Like creatures from another world these haughty Russians came, with their peculiar dress and terrible manners. They were scornful of the West, yet childlike in their amazement at all they saw. And the tsar pretending not to be the tsar—it was too funny!

When Peter reached Holland he could scarcely wait to begin. Using his own tools, he would work with his hands to learn shipbuilding as a carpenter learns it.

Early on the morning following his arrival, he hurried to the shipyard of Zaandam to begin. But the Dutch were wild with curiosity to see this carpenter-tsar. Crowds came by boat and on foot to stare at him. They pushed away the guards and poured into the shipyard. At last Peter was forced to flee to Amsterdam. There he was able to work in peace in the shipyard of the East India Company, closed to the public and surrounded by walls.

Peter didn't want the luxurious house offered to him. He chose instead the master ropemaker's house, where he lived with several of his men. He made his own fire, cooked his meals, and mended his clothes. He even learned to make shoes. Every morning at dawn he set out joyfully to the shipyard dressed as a Dutch workman. He was simply "Carpenter Peter" to them.

After four months, the ship was finished. Peter was given papers that said he was a master of the art of naval architecture. With great pride Peter would thereafter declare, "I, too, am a carpenter!"

From Holland, Peter went to England, where he worked at the Deptford Shipyard. He wandered about the city freely, often dressed in sailor's clothes. Everywhere he went he took his curiosity with him. "What does it do?" he would ask. "How does it work?"

He went into a watchmaker's to have his watch repaired and stayed to learn to take a watch apart and put it together again.

He studied the anatomy of the human body and believed that he was a qualified surgeon, though he limited himself, fortunately, to pulling teeth.

He could not cross a bridge without stopping to see how it was constructed.

Anything that was interesting—and transportable—he shipped back to Russia: microscopes, barometers, a wind dial, an English coffin, even a stuffed crocodile. He hired over eight hundred specialists: engineers, naval officers, doctors, barbers, shipwrights, technicians of all kinds. Peter had to charter ten ships to carry them all. The West was coming to Russia at last.

As Peter's visit drew to a close, King William III of England prepared a grand surprise for him. Knowing Peter's fascination with ships, the king divided his navy into opposing forces and staged a sea battle for him. The ships' cannons did not fire cannonballs, of course, but they gave off smoke and made plenty of noise. Peter watched from the deck of the flagship as the

great vessels maneuvered around one another, playing at war. The English sailors scurried about the decks as Peter watched admiringly. It was all so thrilling to the twenty-five-year-old tsar who had seen his first sailboat only ten years before.

At last Peter was prepared to return home from his great adventure. He had a lot of work to do.

On Peter's arrival, the Russian noblemen gathered at his door to welcome him home. They fell to the floor before their almighty tsar as they had always done. But Peter raised them up.

"You must stop doing that," he said. "If you give such honor to a man, what is left to give to God?"

And then, in a hurry to begin making changes, Peter produced a razor and began removing the noblemen's long beards. To these men their beards were a symbol of their religious belief. God made men with beards; it was therefore a sin to shave them off. No matter! Peter had seen his embassy ridiculed by the Europeans for those beards. It was not modern. It was not the fashion.

He passed a law that all men, except priests and peasants, must shave. If a man insisted on keeping his beard, he could pay a yearly tax on it and wear around his neck, at all times, a bronze medal with a picture of a beard and the words,

"Beards are a ridiculous ornament."

With the beards gone, could those impossible long robes be far behind?

"These things are in your way," he said to his unhappy noblemen, while cutting off their sleeves. "First you knock over a glass, then you dip them in the sauce."

He had them kneel down, and then he cut their robes at the point where they touched the floor. "There," he said. "That's better."

The horrified noblemen looked at the mangled remains of their fine robes—exquisite embroidery cut away, gems hanging loose, priceless heirlooms destroyed.

Soon all men and women were forced by law to dress in the western manner. Pictures of the latest fashions were posted in public places for people to copy.

They didn't like it. They didn't like *any* of it. They wanted things to be the way they had been before. But they might as well have tried to stop the wind as to stop Peter now.

In Europe, Peter had met women who dined and danced with their husbands and even joined them in conversation. He felt ashamed of the women of Russia. Shut away from the world like caged birds, they were ignorant and helpless. By ancient custom Russian women painted their teeth black as a sign of modesty. They did not wear corsets, as European ladies did, and hid their womanly shapes under layers of bulky garments.

Fathers married off their young daughters to men chosen for reasons of business or property. Each daughter was handed over to a stranger, like so much baggage, along with a whip symbolizing the transfer of absolute power to the new husband.

Peter saw that this was wrong and must change. Instead of hiding when their husbands had guests, Peter commanded women to come forward and dine with them. He even arranged parties so that men and women could practice the strange new custom of talking to one another. Young people were not to be forced into arranged marriages anymore, and the bridegroom would no longer carry a whip but offer his bride a kiss instead.

Peter rose at four every day, hours before the sun lit his room. Bursting with energy, he called for his ministers while still in his bedclothes. He often worked fourteen hours a day. There was so much to do!

He was determined that Russia be governed by wise and able men, whether or not of noble birth. So he decreed that any man could serve the government, that everyone must begin at the bottom and work his way up, and that any man who was corrupt or abused his office would be punished savagely, even if he were Peter's closest friend.

But no matter how modern the Russians looked, no matter how well planned their government, unless they were educated they would always be a backward people. Soon books and newspapers popped up everywhere. Schools of mathematics and navigation were built. Peter established an Academy and Museum of Science which was not only free to all: Coffee and wine were served to encourage the people to come.

He built a system of canals, established vineyards, and set up factories of all kinds making new goods for Russia.

Peter dashed from place to place, tirelessly overseeing everything. When a bed was not handy and he needed to rest, he would stretch out on the ground to sleep, using a servant's stomach as a pillow. He wore comfortable old clothes, caring little for luxury. His mind was on something greater: moving, by force if necessary, his beloved country into the modern world.

It was impossible for any country to make so many changes at the same time, and so quickly. But Peter always got what he wanted, and what he wanted most was a modern Russia. He worked hard and made sacrifices; he believed that his countrymen should be willing to do the same.

They were bled dry by taxes and more taxes, for Peter was not only rebuilding Russia: He was also at war with Sweden. As usual, it was the peasants—poor working men and women who owned no land and had few rights—who bore the greatest burden. They had to send their sons to fight in the army for a term of twenty-five years. They had to pay taxes on candles and nuts, boots and hats, horses, beehives, beards, chimneys, and drinking water. Peter had a regular committee whose job it was to think up more taxes.

And what of Peter's greatest dream, the reason he had learned to build ships? Russia must have a navy of her own! Now, at last, he had a place to put it: In the war with Sweden he had captured a marshy strip of land on the Gulf of Finland. And although it was far to the north, freezing cold, and little more than a swampy wilderness, Peter planned to build there, not just a port and a fortress to protect it, but a whole city. It was to be called St. Petersburg after his patron saint, and it would become the new capital of Russia!

Most cities begin as small settlements and grow gradually over hundreds of years. Peter wanted his city overnight. An army of workers was ordered to this frigid, desolate place. There was no wood or stone to build with and no food to feed the workers; everything had to be brought up from Moscow. Because picks and shovels were scarce, in the early years workers were forced to dig the foundations with their bare hands. Through floods in summer and unbearable cold in winter the work went on. Thousands of men lost their lives. The Russians called it a "city built on bones."

Naturally, no one wanted to live on that damp, icy, isolated marsh, so Peter ordered them to come. The royal family, noblemen, and many rich merchants had to leave their comfortable lives in Moscow and build, at their own expense, grand houses in the new city. Simply because Peter wanted it, there grew up out of nothing one of the loveliest cities in the world, a remarkable blend of east and west. With its graceful and majestic buildings in soft yellows and blues and its many bridges joining the nineteen islands to the shore, it is known as the "Venice of the North."

On January 16, 1725, while he was busy with the building of his city, Peter fell ill with an infection and took to his bed. He continued to work at the business of government in his dressing gown, propped up with pillows and anxiously watched by his doctors. Many times Peter had been sick and recovered to work even harder. But now he grew worse and had to send his ministers away. A priest was called to give him the last rites of the church.

"I hope God will forgive me my many sins," Peter whispered, "because of the good I have tried to do for my people."

In the morning chill of January 28, after days of hovering between life and death, Peter died. He was fifty-three years old.

The north wind blew snow in great gusts as a solemn procession carried the coffin to the Fortress Cathedral. As they trudged noiselessly through the snow some must have thought, "Now I can go home to Moscow. And perhaps the taxes will stop." Others surely asked, "How can we go on without him? How could such a man die?"

In the cathedral they prayed for his soul. "O men of Russia!" said the priest. "What is this that we do? The man we lay to rest this day is surely Peter the Great! He has gone, but his work will survive him. He made Russia powerful, and so she will remain."

Though his life was ended and other tsars would sit on his throne, what Peter began went on and on, and Russia was changed forever.